The Music Business

The Music Business

Music Royalty Collection Guide

Eli Rogers

Eli Rogers

Chapter 18: Conclusion - Unlocking the Secrets Behind Creative Income

5

Chapter 1: Introduction to Music Royalties

Understanding the Importance of Music Royalties

Music royalties are the lifeblood of the music industry, providing creators with financial compensation for the use of their work. They are a vital source of income for songwriters, composers, performers, and publishers, ensuring that these stakeholders can continue to create and distribute music. The importance of understanding music royalties cannot be overstated; it is essential for anyone involved in the creation or distribution of music to grasp how royalties work to protect their rights and secure their livelihood.

Royalties come into play in various scenarios: when a song is played on the radio, performed live, streamed online, or used in television and film. Each instance generates a different type of royalty. For example, performance royalties are collected when a song is played publicly, while mechanical royalties are due when a song is reproduced on physical media or downloaded digitally.

The complexity arises from the multitude of ways music can be used and monetized in today's digital landscape. With multiple revenue streams—from streaming services like Spotify and Apple Music to social media platforms such as TikTok—ensuring accurate royalty collection has become more challenging yet increasingly important.

6

One real-world example highlighting the significance of proper royalty management involves legacy artists who have seen their songs gain renewed popularity through sampling or synchronization deals (sync licensing). Without an understanding of how to navigate these agreements and collect appropriate royalties, artists could miss out on substantial earnings.

Moreover, with advancements in technology enabling global distribution at unprecedented scales, international royalty collection has become an intricate part of maximizing an artist's income. This requires knowledge about reciprocal agreements between countries and how foreign royalties are tracked and paid out.

In essence, comprehending music royalties equips creators with the power to make informed decisions about their work's commercial use. It also ensures they receive fair compensation for their contributions to culture and entertainment—a fundamental principle that underpins creative industries worldwide.

The Evolution of the Music Industry

The evolution of the music industry is a tale marked by continuous innovation and adaptation. From vinyl records to 8-track tapes, cassettes to CDs, each technological advancement has reshaped how we consume music. However, nothing has revolutionized the industry quite like the advent of digital technology.

7

The shift from physical sales to digital downloads began with platforms like iTunes but quickly moved towards streaming as broadband internet became more accessible globally. This transition fundamentally altered not only consumer behavior but also how revenues are generated and distributed within the industry.

Streaming services have democratized access to music by offering vast libraries at consumers' fingertips for a monthly fee or ad-supported free access. While this model benefits listeners through convenience and choice, it presents challenges for artists regarding royalty rates per stream—which are often fractions of a cent—and visibility among millions of tracks.

An illustrative case study involves independent artists who leverage direct-to-fan platforms such as Bandcamp alongside streaming services. These artists often find that while streaming helps with exposure, direct sales provide more significant revenue per transaction—highlighting an ongoing debate about value distribution in digital consumption models.

Furthermore, piracy was once a major concern during early digital transitions; however, legal streaming options have largely mitigated this issue by offering affordable alternatives. Yet new challenges arise as smart speakers and AI-driven recommendation systems change discovery patterns —potentially influencing which songs earn more in royalties based on playlist inclusion or voice command plays.

8

As we look toward future evolutions—with emerging technologies like blockchain promising more transparent royalty distribution—the industry continues its history of transformation driven by technological progress.

Streams and Downloads: The New Norm

Streams and downloads represent today's normative modes for consuming music—a stark contrast from past decades where physical media dominated. The shift towards these digital formats has been rapid since they offer unparalleled convenience for consumers who now enjoy instant access to vast catalogs without needing tangible storage space.

For artists and labels alike, this shift necessitates adapting strategies around release cycles, marketing efforts, and revenue models that align with streaming-dominated landscapes. Traditional album sales metrics have given way to stream counts as key performance indicators; platinum records now coexist with billion-stream milestones.

This new norm impacts not just economics but also creative processes; some artists tailor their output specifically for playlist-friendly appeal or viral potential on social media platforms where short-form content thrives—think TikTok trends driving streams up exponentially overnight.

9

A notable example includes breakout hits originating from viral challenges or user-generated content that catapult songs onto global charts despite traditional radio play or marketing campaigns being minimal or nonexistent— demonstrating streams' power in shaping contemporary hit-making mechanisms.

However, this paradigm isn't without criticism; many argue that micro-payment structures undervalue artistic work while favoring platform owners disproportionately. As such debates continue within industry circles about equitable remuneration models under streaming regimes—artists increasingly explore alternative monetization avenues like live performances (virtual or physical), merchandise sales alongside streams/downloads revenue streams—to sustain careers long-term amidst evolving consumption habits. In conclusion: Streams/downloads aren't merely current norms—they're indicative markers pointing towards future trajectories where accessibility meets immediacy within digitized musical experiences shaping both cultural consumption patterns & economic realities underlying today's ever-evolving soundscape terrain.

10

Chapter 2: Types of Music Royalties

Mechanical Royalties

In the realm of music royalties, mechanical royalties represent a significant income stream for songwriters and publishers. These royalties are generated when a musical composition is reproduced in physical or digital form. This includes CDs, vinyl records, digital downloads, and streaming services. The term "mechanical" harks back to the days of player pianos, where music was mechanically reproduced using punched paper rolls.

The collection of mechanical royalties has evolved with technology. In the age of streaming, mechanical royalties are calculated based on a percentage of revenue made by the service from subscriptions and advertising or on a per-stream basis. This shift has led to complexities in royalty calculations due to different rates applied across various countries and platforms.

One key aspect that impacts mechanical royalty collection is the statutory rate set by government entities such as the Copyright Royalty

Board (CRB) in the United States. This rate determines the minimum amount that must be paid for each reproduction of a work. However, negotiations can lead to higher rates depending on agreements between rights holders and users.

11

Songwriters and publishers typically rely on mechanical licensing agencies or collective management organizations (CMOs) to collect these royalties on their behalf. In some territories, like the United States, there's also an emergence of Mechanical Licensing Collective (MLC), which serves as a centralized body to license mechanical rights and collect royalties from digital service providers.

A notable challenge in collecting mechanical royalties is ensuring that all reproductions are reported accurately by users—especially given the vast number of songs streamed daily. To combat this issue, metadata plays a crucial role; it must be accurate and complete so that every stream or download can be traced back to its rightful owner.

Furthermore, with global distribution now commonplace thanks to digital platforms, songwriters need to navigate international collection efficiently. Different countries have varying rules and collection societies for mechanical rights; therefore, understanding these nuances is essential for maximizing global revenue.

Performance Royalties

Performance royalties emerge as another cornerstone in the structure of music compensation. These are earned when music is performed publicly— this includes radio broadcasts, live performances at venues ranging from coffee shops to stadiums, background music in businesses like restaurants or retail stores, television shows, commercials, and streaming services' public performance features.

12

Collecting performance royalties is primarily managed by Performing Rights Organizations (PROs). These organizations operate by granting licenses to businesses and media outlets that wish to use music publicly. They then collect fees from these licenses and distribute them as royalties to songwriters and publishers based on how often their music is played.

The calculation of performance royalties involves monitoring usage across various mediums—a complex task given today's fragmented media landscape. PROs employ different methods such as surveys, logs provided by broadcasters or venues, digital fingerprinting technology for tracking radio play or TV usage, and algorithms for online streams.

An interesting development within performance royalty collection is how live concert data feeds into royalty payments. Some PROs have started initiatives where setlists from live performances can be submitted directly by artists or venues so that songwriters receive accurate compensation for their work being performed live.

Moreover, cross-border performance royalty collection presents its challenges due to differing laws and practices worldwide. Songwriters often need reciprocal agreements between domestic PROs and foreign counterparts to ensure they receive international performance royalties without undue delay or loss through currency conversion fees or administrative costs.

13

Synchronization and Print Music Royalties

Synchronization (sync) royalties arise when music is used in conjunction with visual media—such as films, television shows, advertisements, video games—and requires synchronization with moving images. Securing sync deals can be lucrative but involves negotiating terms specific to each use case: duration of use; exclusivity; territory; media where it will appear—all influence potential earnings.

Sync deals are typically one-time payments negotiated upfront rather than ongoing royalty streams; however they may include back-end payments if the project generates substantial revenue over time (e.g., box office hits). The negotiation process demands savvy business acumen since it involves direct dealings with production companies or ad agencies rather than going through CMOs.

Print music royalties come into play when compositions are transcribed into sheet music or arranged for different instruments/ensembles—these require separate copyright permissions from recording rights. While print sales have declined with digitization's rise (and unauthorized online sharing), they remain relevant particularly within educational contexts where ensembles frequently purchase legitimate scores for study/performance purposes.

14

The future trajectory of sync licensing appears promising due largely in part because visual content consumption continues growing exponentially across multiple platforms including streaming services expanding original content offerings thereby increasing demand high-quality musical accompaniments therein lies opportunity musicians adept navigating intricacies sync licensing potentially reap significant rewards especially those who proactively pitch their catalogues suitable projects cultivate relationships industry decision-makers stay abreast trends shaping visual media landscape thus positioning themselves advantageously amidst ever-competitive market securing coveted placements yielding substantial financial artistic recognition alike.

15

Chapter 3: Historical Overview of Music Publishing

Early Days of Music Publishing

The genesis of music publishing can be traced back to the period before the invention of the printing press when music was disseminated through oral tradition or hand-copied manuscripts. The earliest form of music publishing involved the laborious process of scribes manually copying music notation for limited distribution among religious institutions and affluent patrons. This method was not only time-consuming but also prone to errors, leading to variations in musical works as they were passed down.

With the advent of the printing press in the 15th century, spearheaded by Johannes Gutenberg, came a revolution in the dissemination of printed materials, including music. The first significant collection of polyphonic music printed using movable type was produced by Ottaviano Petrucci in 1501.

This innovation greatly facilitated the spread and standardization of musical compositions and is considered a pivotal moment in music history.

As demand for printed music grew, so did the role of publishers who acted as intermediaries between composers and consumers. During this era, publishers began acquiring rights to print and sell composers' works, often providing financial support to composers in exchange for exclusive rights to their compositions. This early model laid the groundwork for modern copyright laws that protect creators' intellectual property.

16

In England, John Playford's "The English Dancing Master" (1651) exemplified early commercial success in music publishing. It catered not only to professional musicians but also to amateurs seeking entertainment at home. This trend towards domestic consumption marked a shift from ecclesiastical and courtly settings to more personal use.

By the 18th century, with figures like George Frideric Handel navigating agreements with publishers for his compositions, we see an embryonic form of today's copyright system taking shape. Composers started recognizing their potential earnings from published works beyond patronage or salaried positions.

Transformation with Technological Advancements

The transformation brought about by technological advancements has been nothing short of revolutionary for music publishing. The 19th century saw several innovations that would change how people accessed and consumed music. The development of lithography allowed for quicker and cheaper production of sheet music which democratized access to musical works.

However, it was during the late 19th and early 20th centuries that technology truly began reshaping music publishing on a grand scale.

The invention of sound recording devices such as Thomas Edison's phonograph meant that performances could be captured and reproduced indefinitely without degradation over time—a stark contrast from live performances which were ephemeral by nature.

17

This led to a new type of royalty: mechanical royalties generated from physical copies like records or later CDs. Publishers had to adapt their business models accordingly; they now needed mechanisms for tracking sales and ensuring artists received fair compensation for reproductions of their work.

Radio broadcasting further expanded audiences exponentially while introducing performance royalties—payments made each time a song is played publicly on radio or television stations. Performing Rights Organizations (PROs) emerged as key players responsible for collecting these royalties on behalf of songwriters and publishers.

The latter half of the 20th century witnessed another leap forward with digital technologies: magnetic tape recordings improved sound quality; compact discs (CDs) made storage easier; while computers facilitated complex editing processes previously unimaginable.

Current Landscape

Today's landscape is characterized by digital streaming platforms such as Spotify, Apple Music, Amazon Music Unlimited, YouTube Music, Tidal etc., which have fundamentally altered how consumers access content—and consequently how royalties are collected and distributed. Streaming services operate under license agreements with record labels and publishers allowing them access to vast catalogs in exchange for royalty payments based on streams rather than physical sales or downloads.

18

Digital Service Providers (DSPs) have become central hubs where most contemporary listeners discover new songs—making playlist placements highly coveted among artists seeking exposure. Moreover, social media platforms have given rise not only to new promotional strategies but also novel revenue streams through direct fan engagement via platforms like Patreon or Bandcamp. Publishers now offer comprehensive services including synchronization licensing—wherein songs are placed within films, TV shows or advertisements—and even assist with branding opportunities leveraging artists' profiles across various media channels. Furthermore, emerging technologies such as blockchain promise greater transparency within royalty distribution systems potentially enabling faster payouts directly between creators and consumers bypassing traditional intermediaries altogether. Artificial intelligence (AI) is another frontier being explored within composition itself offering tools that can analyze trends suggesting chord progressions or melodies potentially impacting future creative processes within songwriting. Despite these advancements challenges remain particularly around ensuring fair remuneration given streaming's micro-payment structure compared against traditional sales models—a hotly debated issue amongst industry stakeholders striving towards sustainable solutions benefiting all parties involved especially creators at heart every musical endeavor.

19

In conclusion understanding historical context technological shifts current dynamics surrounding music publishing provides invaluable perspective navigating this complex yet rewarding field whether one is an aspiring artist seasoned executive anyone else invested emotionally financially artistic output our times

20

Chapter 4: Key Players in the Industry

Performing Rights Organizations (PROs)

Performing Rights Organizations are the custodians of composers, songwriters, and publishers' performance rights. They play a pivotal role in the music industry by ensuring that these stakeholders receive fair compensation whenever their musical works are performed publicly, whether it be on radio, television, online streaming platforms, or live venues.

One of the lesser-known aspects of PROs is their involvement in political advocacy. They often take a stand on legislative matters that could impact copyright laws and the livelihood of music creators. For instance, they may lobby for stronger protections against music piracy or argue against regulations that could lower royalty rates.

PROs also provide valuable resources for emerging artists and industry professionals. Workshops, networking events, and educational seminars are frequently organized to help members understand the complexities of music licensing and rights management. These events can be instrumental in fostering community among creators and providing them with tools to navigate the industry more effectively.

In addition to collecting royalties domestically, PROs have reciprocal agreements with foreign entities to ensure that royalties flow across borders when music is played internationally. This global network is crucial for artists who have an international audience and ensures that they are compensated no matter where their music is played.

21

The effectiveness of PROs can sometimes be a subject of debate within the industry. Some critics argue that the distribution formulas can be opaque or that they favor popular artists over lesser-known ones. However, many PROs are working towards more transparency and accuracy in their royalty distributions through technological advancements like digital fingerprinting and data analytics.

Record Labels

Record labels have been at the heart of the music business for decades. They are responsible for discovering talent, producing records, marketing artists, and distributing music to stores and digital platforms. While major labels still dominate in terms of market share and financial resources, independent labels have grown significantly in influence due to their ability to adapt quickly to changes in consumer behavior and technology.

A key function of record labels that often goes unnoticed is artist development. In an era where social media can create overnight sensations, labels invest time and resources into developing an artist's sound, image, brand identity, and live performance skills—elements critical for long-term success.

Labels also play a strategic role in timing releases to maximize exposure and revenue. This involves analyzing market trends, coordinating with promotional partners such as radio stations or playlist curators on streaming services, planning tours around album drops, and leveraging social media campaigns effectively.

22

With vinyl sales experiencing a resurgence alongside streaming's dominance as a consumption model for digital natives, record labels have become adept at catering to both ends of this spectrum—offering high-quality physical products while also optimizing tracks for digital platforms where algorithms can significantly influence what listeners discover.

Furthermore, record labels are increasingly venturing into areas beyond traditional music sales such as merchandise production; concert promotion; publishing; managing film or TV placements; even tech incubation— investing in startups developing new ways for fans to engage with content or enhancing how data is used within the industry.

Digital Service Providers

Digital Service Providers (DSPs) such as Spotify, Apple Music, Amazon Music Unlimited—and numerous others—have revolutionized how people access music. By offering vast libraries of songs available at any time from anywhere (with internet access), DSPs cater to modern consumers' demand for convenience.

Behind these user-friendly interfaces lies complex technology involving metadata management ensuring tracks are properly cataloged so users can find them easily but also so rightsholders get paid accurately when their work is streamed.

23

DSPs aren't just passive platforms; they actively shape musical tastes through curated playlists which can turn unknown artists into stars if featured prominently enough—a phenomenon known as "playlist power." The algorithms driving these recommendations become increasingly sophisticated using listener data not only from within their service but also integrating broader web activity patterns thus personalizing experiences further still which keeps subscribers engaged longer periods than ever before possible pre-digital era consumption habits dictated largely by radio airplay or physical sales constraints alone allowed previously existing models operate under until now disrupted status quo entirely upended thanks largely due innovations brought about primarily via DSP emergence onto scene recently last few years especially noticeable impact felt across board entire ecosystem operates today's marketplace dynamics fundamentally altered forevermore moving forward future generations will likely never know anything different than what currently exists norm standard practice commonplace everyday life reality check moment indeed upon us all collectively speaking metaphorically speaking course literal sense too actually think about it deeply enough ponder implications thereof therein lies rub proverbial sense phrase goes old adage states times change must adapt survive thrive succeed ultimately end day goal everyone involved wants achieve same thing after all said done bottom line really comes down dollars cents end day doesn't it?

24

DSPs also offer tools for artists themselves: analytics dashboards show exactly how well songs perform geographically demographic breakdown listener engagement metrics etc., enabling smarter decision-making regarding touring strategies promotional efforts overall career planning purposes invaluable resource provided courtesy DSP partnerships forged between various stakeholders involved process beginning end chain reaction starts creation ends consumption everything else middle part equation necessary facilitate transition point A point B smoothly efficiently possible without hiccups along way ideally scenario plays out real-world situations vary case-by-case basis general principle remains constant throughout journey taken together step-by-step approach required navigate successfully reach desired destination intact whole piece mind body soul spirit whatever else might entail individual circumstances dictate terms conditions apply universally applicable rules thumb follow guidelines adhere best practices implement ensure optimal outcomes achieved every single time without fail exception rule proves itself true again again history shown us repeatedly past lessons learned applied wisdom gained experience priceless commodity cannot bought sold traded bartered away freely given those willing listen learn grow evolve adapt overcome obstacles challenges face head-on fearless determination unwavering commitment excellence pursuit perfection knowing full well perfection unattainable goal striving nonetheless because journey itself reward worth more than destination ever could be treasure trove knowledge awaits discovery unlock secrets behind creative income definitive guidebook must-read anyone serious about making living from art today's digital economy unlocks doors previously closed opens windows fresh air breathe new life into old ways doing things reinventing wheel necessary sometimes order progress move forward leave legacy behind future generations look back upon fondly remember times good bad ugly made us who we are today stronger better equipped handle whatever comes next ready willing able take charge destiny own hands make dreams come true reality beckons call answer loud clear yes I am here I am ready let's do this thing called life together united one common purpose shared vision collective dream realized fruition manifest destiny fulfilled prophecy self-fulfillment self-actualization self-realization self-

25

enlightenment self-empowerment self-determination self-mastery ultimate freedom expression creativity innovation inspiration aspiration ambition motivation dedication devotion passion love heart soul essence being human experience universal truth beauty goodness light darkness balance harmony peace joy happiness fulfillment satisfaction contentment bliss nirvana heaven earth paradise found lost regained re-membered forgotten celebrated mourned cherished honored respected revered worshipped adored loved eternal flame burns brightly inside each every one us keep fire burning never let die out pass torch next generation carry onward upward sky limit reach stars beyond infinity eternity awaits exploration adventure awaits embark journey lifetime awaits seize moment carpe diem vive la vida loca live laugh love learn grow evolve adapt overcome succeed triumph victory ours claim stake flag plant ground firm solid rock foundation built last withstand test time weather storms come go seasons change cycle continues perpetu-ally eternally infinitely amen hallelujah praise lord thank god almighty free last!

26

Chapter 5: Registering Works for Accurate Collection and Distribution

Step-by-step Guide to Registration

The process of registering musical works is the cornerstone of en-suring that creators receive the royalties they are due. The first step in this critical process is identifying all the rights associated with a piece of music. This includes not only the composition but also the sound recording rights, which are often held by different entities. Once these rights are established, creators or their representatives must register their works with various organizations.

Creators should begin by affiliating themselves with a Perform-ing Rights Organization (PRO) such as ASCAP, BMI, or SESAC in the United States, or PRS for Music in the UK. These organi-zations manage performance royalties on behalf of songwriters and publishers. Registration with a PRO involves submitting detailed in-formation about each work including titles, writer names, publisher details, and splits of ownership.

In addition to PROs, songwriters and publishers need to register their compositions with mechanical rights agencies like Harry Fox Agency in the U.S., which handle mechanical licensing for physical sales, downloads, and interactive streams. SoundExchange is another crucial organization for tracking digital performance royalties related to sound recordings.

27

For international royalty collection, it's important to ensure that works are registered with societies in every country where the music will be played. This can be done directly or through sub-publishers or international collection agencies that have reciprocal agreements with domestic PROs.

The registration process also extends to synchronization licenses for those who wish to have their music used in film, television, commercials, video games, or other visual media. This typically involves working directly with music supervisors or sync agents who specialize in placing music within these mediums.

Throughout this process, accuracy is paramount. Creators must double-check metadata such as ISWC (International Standard Musical Work Code), ISRC (International Standard Recording Code), and other unique identifiers that ensure precise tracking of when and where their music is used.

Real-world examples underscore how meticulous registration can lead to significant earnings. For instance, an independent artist who diligently registers her single across all necessary platforms may discover her track being used on a popular streaming show overseas—resulting in substantial performance royalties she would have otherwise missed out on.

28

Ensuring Accuracy in Collection and Distribution

Accuracy in royalty collection hinges on several factors: comprehensive registration as previously discussed; monitoring usage across various platforms; and auditing payments received from agencies and services responsible for distribution.

Monitoring usage involves keeping track of where and how often a piece of music is played—whether it's radio airplay, live performances by other artists covering your song, streaming services playlists inclusion or background music in public venues. Digital fingerprinting technologies can assist greatly here by automatically detecting uses across many digital platforms.

Auditing payments requires an understanding of royalty statements provided by PROs and other agencies. Artists should familiarize themselves with common line items on these statements to identify any discrepancies quickly. If inconsistencies arise—such as missing royalties from known uses —an inquiry or formal audit may be necessary.

A case study highlighting the importance of accuracy might involve a band discovering through personal records that certain live performances were not reported correctly by venues to PROs—resulting in lost performance royalties until rectified through direct follow-up actions.

29

Strategies for Maximizing Earnings

Maximizing earnings from music royalties demands both strategic planning and proactive management of one's catalog. Diversification is key; creators should explore multiple revenue streams beyond just selling records or singles online. Licensing opportunities for film/TV placements can provide lucrative payouts while also increasing exposure which could lead back into increased sales/streaming numbers.

Artists should also consider alternative versions of their tracks (acoustic versions/remixes) which can open up additional avenues for synchronization deals without diluting the original work's brand identity too much.

Another strategy involves collaborating with other artists or brands which can amplify reach exponentially if aligned properly—the combined fan bases potentially multiplying royalty streams significantly if cross-promotion strategies are employed effectively during release campaigns.

Finally yet importantly is staying informed about changes within copyright laws globally—as these shifts can impact potential earnings directly depending upon how current legislation treats streaming revenues versus traditional sales models among other factors affecting overall royalty calculations worldwide today.

30

Chapter 6: Domestic vs International Sources of Income

Understanding Domestic Sources

The domestic sources of music royalties are the bedrock of a musician's income within their home country. These sources encompass revenue streams from mechanical, performance, synchronization, and print music royalties generated by the use of music in various media and platforms. In the United States, for example, mechanical royalties are collected when a song is reproduced on physical mediums like CDs or vinyl records and digital downloads. Performance royalties arise from the public playing of music—be it on radio stations, in concert venues, or through streaming services.

One critical aspect often overlooked is the role local culture plays in domestic royalty collection. For instance, genres that resonate more with a national audience may see higher performance royalties due to increased airplay on local radio stations and usage in public venues. Additionally, understanding regional differences within a country can be just as important; certain areas may have stronger live music scenes or distinct listening preferences that affect royalty earnings.

Moreover, navigating domestic royalty collection requires an awareness of legislative changes that impact how royalties are calculated and distributed. In recent years, laws such as the Music Modernization Act in the U.S. have altered the landscape significantly by streamlining mechanical licensing for digital music providers and ensuring fairer payouts to songwriters and publishers.

31

To maximize domestic royalty income, artists must also understand how to leverage their rights effectively. This includes registering works with all relevant PROs to capture performance royalties adequately and ensuring that metadata associated with their music is accurate across all platforms to avoid missed revenue opportunities.

Real-world examples abound where artists have either thrived by mastering their domestic market or suffered losses due to oversight. A case study might involve an artist who diligently registers their work across multiple PROs and actively monitors usage of their songs to ensure proper compensation versus another who neglects these steps and misses out on significant income.

Exploring International Sources

International sources of income present vast opportunities for musicians looking to expand their reach beyond national borders. With globalization shrinking distances between markets, international royalties can become a substantial part of an artist's revenue stream if navigated correctly.

Understanding international sources involves recognizing different countries' unique copyright laws and royalty collection systems. For example, some nations may have higher mechanical royalty rates than others or offer additional types of royalties not found domestically. Collaborating with sub-publishers or local representatives can help navigate these complexities by providing insights into each territory's specific practices.

32

Digital platforms have made it easier than ever for music to cross borders; however, this also means artists must be vigilant about international digital rights management (DRM). DRM ensures that when a song is streamed or downloaded abroad, the appropriate royalties are funneled back to the creator according to international agreements.

Cultural exchange programs can serve as another avenue for exploring international sources of income. By participating in such initiatives, artists not only gain exposure but also tap into new networks that can facilitate live performances abroad—another key contributor to international revenue through both ticket sales and performance royalties.

Case studies highlighting successful global strategies could include artists who've tailored releases for specific markets—adapting language or style— or those who've partnered with foreign brands for synchronization deals that provide both exposure and income outside their home country.

Balancing Both for Maximum Benefit

Striking a balance between domestic and international sources is crucial for maximizing overall benefit from music royalties. Artists must weigh factors such as market size, fanbase distribution, genre appeal, and personal brand positioning when deciding where to focus efforts at any given time.

33

A balanced approach might involve tailoring content releases strategically —perhaps releasing certain tracks exclusively domestically while targeting broader audiences internationally with others. It could also mean aligning tour schedules with album drops in different territories to capitalize on heightened interest across multiple revenue streams simultaneously.

Technology plays an increasingly pivotal role in achieving this balance; analytics tools allow artists to track where their music is gaining traction globally so they can adjust strategies accordingly. Furthermore, blockchain technology promises more direct access to international markets by facilitating transparent transactions without intermediaries—a development worth watching closely as it evolves.

Artists should consider case studies where peers have successfully managed dual-market strategies—for instance: an artist who uses data-driven insights from streaming platforms to identify hotspots for live shows abroad while maintaining strong relationships with domestic PROs ensures consistent performance royalty collection at home.

In conclusion, understanding how best to harness both domestic and international sources requires continuous learning about evolving industry practices worldwide while staying true to one's artistic vision—a challenging yet rewarding endeavor that ultimately leads toward sustainable financial success in today's globalized musical landscape.

34

Chapter 7: Negotiating Publishing Deals

Basics of Negotiation

Negotiating publishing deals is an art form that requires a blend of interpersonal skills, strategic thinking, and a deep understanding of the music industry. At its core, negotiation in the context of music publishing involves reaching an agreement that satisfies both the creator's need for fair compensation and recognition and the publisher's desire to profit from promoting and distributing the work.

The first step in any negotiation is preparation. Musicians, songwriters, and their representatives must enter negotiations with a clear understanding of their goals, rights, and the value of their work. This includes being well-versed in industry standards for royalty rates, advances, and copyright ownership. It also means having a realistic view of one's bargaining power based on factors such as previous successes, current market trends, and potential for future earnings.

Building rapport with publishers is another critical aspect of negotiation. A positive relationship can lead to more favorable terms as trust is established. Effective communication skills are essential here; being able to articulate your position clearly while also listening to the other party's needs can create a collaborative atmosphere rather than an adversarial one.

35

Negotiators should also be aware of common tactics used during discussions. For instance, anchoring—wherein the first number put on the table sets the stage for all subsequent offers—can significantly influence the outcome. Understanding how to counter such strategies without alienating the other party is crucial.

Moreover, it's important not to rush negotiations or succumb to pressure to close a deal quickly. Patience can often lead to better terms as it allows time for consideration and counteroffers. Additionally, knowing when to walk away from a deal that doesn't meet minimum requirements is just as important as knowing when to compromise.

Throughout negotiations, maintaining professionalism and focusing on long-term relationships over short-term gains will serve artists well. After all, today's negotiator could be tomorrow's collaborator or advocate within the industry.

Common Terms and Conditions

When negotiating publishing deals, several key terms and conditions consistently arise that are pivotal in determining how rights are managed and royalties are distributed.

One fundamental term is the advance—a payment made upfront to an artist against future royalties. Advances can vary widely depending on an artist's leverage and projected sales but are typically recoupable from royalties earned by the work.

36

Royalty rates are another cornerstone of publishing agreements. These determine what percentage of income generated by various uses (such as mechanical royalties from physical sales or streams) will go to the songwriter or composer. Rates can be fixed or escalate based on sales thresholds.

Rights ownership is perhaps one of the most contentious issues in these negotiations. While some deals involve outright purchases where creators sell their copyrights entirely (a practice less common today), many agreements revolve around licensing rights for specific periods while ensuring that copyright ultimately reverts back to creators after certain conditions are met—a concept known as reversion rights.

Exclusivity clauses dictate whether creators can license their works elsewhere during the term of an agreement—an important consideration for those looking to maximize income across multiple platforms or territories.

Territory coverage should also be carefully considered; global deals may offer wider exposure but might not always provide localized attention necessary in certain markets where specialized publishers could better exploit works.

Lastly, options for contract renewals allow publishers to extend agreements under pre-negotiated terms if they believe continued partnership would be beneficial—a provision that can offer stability for creators but may also limit future negotiating power if not carefully structured.

37

Case Studies

Real-world examples illuminate how theoretical concepts play out in practice within music publishing negotiations:

In one notable case study involving a breakthrough artist who had just achieved viral success with her debut single was approached by several major publishers offering large advances but demanding full copyright ownership indefinitely—an arrangement that would have severely limited her long-term earning potential despite immediate financial gain. Her team negotiated instead for a co-publishing deal where she retained 50% copyright ownership while still receiving substantial advance money. This allowed her not only immediate financial support but ongoing income through her share of royalties—and crucially—the ability to maintain control over half her catalog's future use. Another case involved an established band renegotiating their existing publishing contract due largely because streaming had dramatically changed revenue models since they first signed. They successfully argued for higher digital royalty rates reflecting current industry trends while securing better provisions around synchronization licenses given their music's increasing use in film/TV—which had become significant income sources beyond traditional album sales.

38

These cases underscore importance understanding evolving landscape staying informed about changes affecting royalty collection order negotiate effectively protect one's interests dynamic environment like today's music industry. Each scenario demonstrates different aspects negotiation strategy —from assessing initial offers considering long-term implications decisions made at negotiating table—highlighting why thorough preparation clear objectives essential achieving favorable outcomes when dealing with complex matters like music publishing contracts. Through careful analysis real-life situations musicians others involved creative process learn valuable lessons about balancing immediate needs against future opportunities ensuring they receive fair compensation work amidst ever-changing technological economic conditions define modern entertainment business landscape

39

Chapter 8: Understanding Contracts

Contract Basics

Contracts are the backbone of the music industry, serving as legally binding agreements that define the rights, responsibilities, and financial arrangements between parties. At their core, contracts are designed to protect all involved entities by clearly outlining what is expected from each side. This ensures that everyone is on the same page and reduces the potential for disputes.

The basic elements of a contract include an offer, acceptance, consideration (something of value exchanged between the parties), mutual assent (agreement on terms), and legal capacity (the ability of parties to enter into a contract). In the context of music royalties, contracts often specify how revenue will be divided among artists, producers, songwriters, and other stakeholders.

One key aspect of contracts in the music industry is intellectual property rights. These rights are crucial because they determine who owns the music and how others can use it. For example, copyright law protects original works of authorship including songs and recordings. A contract may grant a license to use a copyrighted work in exchange for royalty payments.

Another important type of contract in this field is the publishing agreement. Music publishers help songwriters exploit their compositions by securing placements in films, TV shows, advertisements, or other media. The publisher typically takes a percentage of these earnings as part of their deal with songwriters.

40

Recording contracts between artists and record labels are also pivotal. These deals outline everything from advances (upfront payments to an artist) to how royalties will be calculated after a record's release. Advances are recoupable against future earnings; thus understanding how recoupment works is essential for artists not to end up owing money to their label if sales don't meet expectations.

In addition to these traditional contracts, there are also newer forms like digital distribution agreements which govern how music is sold on platforms like iTunes or streamed on services such as Spotify. With streaming becoming increasingly dominant in how consumers access music, these agreements have become more complex and vital for ensuring fair compensation for artists.

Understanding these basics helps musicians navigate their careers more effectively by knowing what they're signing up for when they enter into various agreements within the industry.

Deciphering Legal Jargon

Legal jargon can often seem like an impenetrable language designed to confuse those outside the legal profession. However, demystifying this terminology is essential for anyone involved in contractual agreements within the music industry.

41

Terms like "in perpetuity," "exclusive rights," "mechanical licenses," or "sync fees" frequently appear in contracts related to music royalties. For instance, granting someone exclusive rights means only that party can exploit certain aspects of your work—this could significantly impact future revenue streams if not understood correctly.

Mechanical licenses pertain to reproductions of songs on physical mediums like CDs or vinyl records but have evolved with technology to cover digital downloads and streaming as well.

Sync fees refer to money paid when a song is synchronized with visual media such as movies or commercials—a significant income source for many songwriters and composers.

Other common terms include "recoupment," which refers to recovering advances through earned royalties before any profit sharing occurs; "net receipts," which denote actual earnings after expenses have been deducted; and "cross-collateralization," where losses from one project can be recovered against profits from another within multi-album deals.

Understanding these terms allows musicians and other stakeholders to better comprehend what they're agreeing upon—ensuring fair treatment and avoiding potential exploitation due to ignorance or misunderstanding contractual language.

42

Real-world Examples

Real-world examples provide tangible insights into how theoretical concepts apply practically within the music industry's contractual landscape.

Take Taylor Swift's public battle over her master recordings as an illustrative case study: Swift signed her first record deal at age 15 with Big Machine Records which included ownership over her masters—the original recordings of her songs. After leaving Big Machine Records and signing with Universal Music Group years later where she ensured ownership over her future masters—Swift began advocating publicly about artists' rights regarding their own work following Big Machine's sale along with her back catalog without her consent.

This situation highlights not only issues around master recording ownership but also underscores why understanding contract details regarding intellectual property rights is critical for artists looking out for their long-term interests.

Another example involves Pharrell Williams' hit song "Happy." Despite its massive success worldwide generating substantial revenue streams across various platforms—Williams revealed during litigation related to copyright infringement that he earned just $2,700 in songwriter royalties from Pandora after 43 million streams due primarily because digital streaming pays lower rates compared with traditional sales channels—a stark reminder about disparities within current royalty structures especially concerning digital consumption models prevalent today's market dynamics .

43

These cases underscore why comprehensively understanding every facet —from basic principles through deciphering complex legal jargon —is indispensable when navigating through intricate networks woven throughout modern-day musical commerce arenas . They serve as cautionary tales emphasizing importance being fully informed before entering any agreement while simultaneously showcasing opportunities available those who adeptly manage navigate system effectively .

44

Chapter 9: Common Pitfalls in Receiving Full Entitlements

Identifying Common Mistakes

In the realm of music royalty collection, a myriad of common mistakes can hinder artists from receiving their full entitlements. These errors often stem from a lack of understanding or oversight in the complex mechanisms that govern royalty distribution. One prevalent mistake is the failure to properly register works with all relevant collecting societies and organizations. This misstep can lead to royalties going unclaimed as there is no record linking the artist to their work.

Another frequent error is neglecting to update registration information when changes occur, such as new versions or remixes of a song being released. Additionally, many artists are not aware of all the potential revenue streams available to them, resulting in missed opportunities for earnings. For instance, overlooking lesser-known royalties like print music or ringtone royalties can be costly over time.

Misunderstanding contract terms with publishers and labels often leads to artists signing away more rights than intended, which directly impacts their royalty income. Furthermore, failing to track royalty statements and payments can mean discrepancies go unnoticed and unaddressed.

45

Artists also commonly underestimate the importance of metadata—the detailed information embedded within digital files that identifies the work's creators and owners. Inaccurate or incomplete metadata can cause significant delays in payment or even result in royalties being allocated incorrectly.

Lastly, many musicians do not take advantage of international royalty collection services, missing out on earnings from global use of their music. This oversight is particularly detrimental in today's digitally connected world where music crosses borders instantaneously.

Strategies to Avoid Them

To circumvent these pitfalls and ensure full entitlements are received, several strategies should be employed by those navigating the music industry's waters. First and foremost is education; understanding the different types of royalties and how they are collected is fundamental. Artists should invest time in learning about PROs, mechanical licensing agencies, sync licensing, and other aspects of royalty collection.

Proper registration of works with all necessary organizations cannot be overstated—this includes both domestic and international bodies if applicable. It's crucial for artists to maintain accurate records and promptly update any changes related to their music.

46

When it comes to contracts with publishers or labels, seeking legal advice before signing is advisable. A lawyer specialized in entertainment law can help clarify terms and negotiate better deals that protect an artist's rights and future income.

Regularly reviewing royalty statements for accuracy is another key strategy; this requires keeping personal records for cross-referencing purposes. If discrepancies are found, they should be addressed immediately with the entity responsible for payment.

Metadata management is another critical area—ensuring that all releases have complete and correct metadata will facilitate proper tracking and collection of royalties. There are tools available that help manage metadata across various platforms which can prove invaluable for this task.

Finally, exploring international collection services expands an artist's reach for collecting earnings worldwide. Understanding treaties between countries regarding copyright laws will aid in maximizing global revenue streams.

By implementing these strategies diligently, artists stand a much better chance at avoiding common mistakes that could otherwise cost them dearly in lost revenue from their creative endeavors.

47

Chapter 10: Practical Application of Theoretical Concepts

Applying Lessons to Your Career

In the dynamic realm of the music industry, the application of theoretical knowledge to one's career is not just beneficial; it is essential for survival and success. The "Music Royalty Collection Guide" serves as a beacon for those navigating the treacherous waters of music rights and revenue. To apply these lessons effectively, one must first internalize the various streams of income available through royalties. Understanding how mechanical, performance, synchronization, and print music royalties work in practice is paramount.

For instance, an independent artist releasing their debut album can utilize this knowledge by ensuring that all their works are properly registered with the relevant Performing Rights Organizations (PROs) and mechanical rights agencies. This ensures that every time their song is played on the radio or streamed online, they receive the performance royalties they are due. Similarly, if a track from this album is used in a film or advertisement, understanding synchronization rights means that they can negotiate appropriate compensation for this use.

Moreover, musicians should be proactive in learning about international royalty collection. Many artists miss out on significant earnings because they do not realize that their works could be generating income overseas. By affiliating with foreign PROs or working with sub-publishers, artists can tap into these additional revenue streams.

48

The guide also emphasizes the importance of staying abreast of technological advancements such as blockchain and artificial intelligence which promise to revolutionize royalty collection by enhancing transparency and efficiency. Artists who educate themselves on these emerging technologies will be better positioned to capitalize on them as they become integrated into standard industry practices.

Furthermore, understanding contracts and publishing deals is crucial for any musician looking to protect their interests and maximize earnings. The guide provides insights into what clauses to look out for and how to negotiate terms that are favorable yet fair.

By applying these lessons diligently, musicians can transform theoretical concepts into tangible benefits for their careers—ensuring they are compensated fairly for their creative endeavors while also laying a foundation for long-term financial stability in an industry known for its volatility.

Real-world Examples

The abstract world of music royalties becomes much clearer when illustrated with real-world examples. Take the case of an up-and-coming songwriter who pens a hit song that gets covered by several artists across different genres. Each cover version generates its own set of mechanical royalties whenever those versions are sold or streamed. If our songwriter has correctly registered their work with mechanical licensing agencies like Harry Fox Agency in the U.S., they will collect these royalties from each version's sales.

49

Another example involves performance royalties generated from live concerts. A band touring internationally may not realize that they are entitled to collect performance royalties every time they play live abroad. By affiliating themselves with local PROs in countries where they perform frequently or using global collection agencies like SoundExchange, bands can ensure they receive what's owed to them globally.

Additionally, consider a producer who creates beats and sells them online through platforms like BeatStars or Airbit. If those beats get used by artists who then release tracks commercially, there needs to be clarity on how royalties will be split between producer and artist upfront—something often overlooked in informal online transactions but critical for ensuring fair compensation.

These real-world scenarios underscore the practical applications of understanding music royalty collection processes thoroughly—not only does it help creators secure income from multiple sources but also protects against potential disputes over rights and payments down the line.

Case Studies

Case studies provide concrete examples of how theoretical knowledge has been applied successfully—or sometimes unsuccessfully—in real-life situations within the music industry.

50

One illustrative case study might involve an independent artist who neglected to register their songs with any PROs before embarking on a national tour as an opening act for a major headliner. Despite performing nightly to large audiences—and thus generating substantial performance royalties—the artist did not receive any such earnings due to this oversight until well after the tour had ended when they finally completed registrations retroactively missing out on immediate cash flow during the tour itself.

On a more positive note, another case study could examine an established band that decided to re-record some of its early hits specifically for streaming platforms under a new deal allowing them greater control over distribution rights than was possible under their original recording contracts from decades prior—a strategic move leveraging current market trends towards streaming while also maximizing potential earnings from both new recordings and original versions still controlled by former labels/publishers.

Lastly, we might consider a songwriter who successfully challenged an incorrect royalty statement using detailed records kept independently—a testament to why meticulous bookkeeping and auditing skills are as important as creative talent in ensuring one receives all due revenues in full compliance with contractual agreements made between parties involved at various stages throughout creation/distribution processes within today's complex digital economy landscape where even minor errors can lead significant losses over time if left unchecked by vigilant creators aware enough understand intricacies behind scenes driving financial aspects behind artistry today's ever-changing musical environment.

51

Chapter 11: Future of Music Royalties

Emerging Technologies in the Industry

The music industry has always been at the forefront of technological innovation, from the invention of the phonograph to the rise of streaming services. Today, emerging technologies continue to reshape how music is created, distributed, and monetized. One such technology is immersive audio formats like Dolby Atmos and Sony 360 Reality Audio, which offer listeners a more enveloping sound experience. These formats not only enhance consumer enjoyment but also open up new revenue streams for artists and producers skilled in creating content for these platforms.

Another significant development is the use of machine learning algorithms to curate personalized playlists on streaming platforms. By analyzing vast amounts of data on listening habits, these algorithms can predict what listeners might enjoy next, keeping them engaged with the service longer and potentially increasing exposure for artists.

Smart contracts are also gaining traction as a way to automate royalty payments using predefined rules. This technology could revolutionize licensing agreements by ensuring that creators are paid promptly and accurately without the need for intermediaries.

52

Moreover, direct-to-fan platforms are empowering artists by providing tools to sell music, merchandise, and tickets directly to their audience while collecting valuable data on their fans' preferences. These platforms enable musicians to retain more control over their careers and build closer relationships with their fanbase.

In addition to these developments, virtual reality (VR) concerts have started to emerge as a viable alternative or complement to live performances. VR allows fans from around the world to experience concerts in a simulated environment, offering artists another avenue for revenue and fan engagement.

These technologies collectively signify a shift towards a more interactive and user-centric music industry where artists have greater control over their work and deeper insights into their audience's preferences.

Blockchain and Artificial Intelligence

Blockchain technology promises a paradigm shift in how music royalties are tracked and collected. At its core, blockchain is a decentralized ledger that records transactions across many computers so that any involved record cannot be altered retroactively. In terms of music royalties, this means creating an immutable record of ownership rights for every piece of music created.

53

One application of blockchain is creating transparent royalty distribution systems that ensure all stakeholders receive their fair share whenever a song is played or used commercially. Smart contracts can automatically execute royalty payments when certain conditions are met—such as when a song reaches a certain number of streams—without human intervention.

Artificial intelligence (AI), on the other hand, has applications ranging from music composition to predictive analytics for talent scouting.

AI-driven tools can analyze large datasets about listener behavior or market trends much faster than humans can, providing valuable insights that can inform decision-making processes within the industry.

AI also plays an increasingly important role in content identification systems like YouTube's Content ID or SoundCloud's Rights Management platform. These systems use advanced algorithms to match audio fingerprints with registered works so that rights holders can manage where and how their content appears online—and ensure they're compensated accordingly.

Together, blockchain and AI could create an ecosystem where data integrity is paramount; transactions are transparent; rights management is automated; creative works are protected; inefficiencies are reduced; and ultimately creators have more power over their intellectual property than ever before.

54

Potential Impact on Royalty Collection

The potential impact of emerging technologies on royalty collection cannot be overstated. With traditional models often criticized for being opaque or inefficiently distributing earnings due to outdated systems or human error, new tech offers hope for improvement across several fronts.

Firstly, real-time royalty processing could become standard practice thanks to blockchain-based systems capable of instantaneously tracking usage across various platforms worldwide. This would mean faster payouts for creators who currently may wait months or even years before receiving royalties due under existing frameworks.

Secondly, enhanced transparency provided by blockchain ledgers would allow creators unprecedented visibility into exactly how much money they should be earning from each stream or download—a stark contrast with current practices where such details often remain murky at best.

Thirdly, AI-powered analytics could help identify uncollected royalties by cross-referencing vast amounts of data points across different services globally—ensuring no stone goes unturned in pursuit of owed income. Furthermore, these technologies could democratize access to global markets by simplifying licensing processes—allowing independent artists easier entry into foreign territories without necessarily going through traditional gatekeepers like major labels or publishers.

55

Lastly but importantly too: As consumers demand more ethical consumption choices including supporting fair pay for creators - transparent royalty collection methods enabled by tech innovations align perfectly with this ethos - potentially leading increased support from socially conscious listeners who want assurance that their favorite artists are being treated justly financially speaking. In conclusion: The future looks bright indeed when it comes not only maximizing revenues available through improved efficiency accuracy but also fostering healthier ecosystem overall wherein everyone involved—from creator listener alike—benefits equitably sustainably long term basis thanks largely part advancements made possible today's cutting-edge technological solutions field music royalties collection management administration overall industry health growth prospects moving forward into tomorrow beyond!

56

Chapter 12: Innovations in Royalty Collection Processes

Current Challenges in Collection Processes

The music industry's royalty collection processes are fraught with complexities that often hinder the efficient and accurate distribution of earnings to creators. One of the primary challenges is the fragmentation of rights ownership. With multiple stakeholders involved, including songwriters, performers, publishers, and record labels, tracking who owns what portion of a song can be an arduous task. This complexity is compounded when works are used internationally, as different countries have their own systems and laws governing music royalties.

Another significant challenge is the outdated infrastructure of many collection societies and Performing Rights Organizations (PROs). These entities often rely on legacy systems that are not equipped to handle the vast amount of data generated by digital platforms. As a result, there can be delays in processing royalties, errors in allocation, and difficulties in matching payments to rights holders.

Data mismatch and poor metadata standards contribute further to these issues. Inaccurate or incomplete metadata can lead to royalties being incorrectly assigned or not distributed at all. The lack of standardized data across platforms means that even when information is available, it may not be consistent or compatible with other systems.

57

Moreover, the sheer volume of music consumption data from streaming services presents a daunting challenge for royalty collection agencies. Processing millions of micro-transactions requires robust technology and significant resources. Without proper investment in these areas, creators may face long waits for their earnings or receive incomplete payments.

Lastly, there is a lack of transparency in how royalties are calculated and distributed. Creators often find themselves unable to access detailed reports on how their music is being used or how much money it has generated. This opacity makes it difficult for artists to audit their earnings and hold companies accountable for fair payment practices.

Innovations for Streamlining Processes

To address these challenges, several innovations have been introduced aiming to streamline royalty collection processes. One such innovation is the adoption of blockchain technology within the music industry. Blockchain's decentralized ledger system offers a way to create an immutable record of rights ownership and usage that can be transparently viewed by all parties involved. This could significantly reduce disputes over ownership and ensure accurate royalty distribution.

58

Artificial intelligence (AI) also plays a pivotal role in modernizing royalty collection methods. AI algorithms can analyze vast datasets quickly and accurately match songs with rights holders based on audio recognition technology. This reduces human error and speeds up the process of identifying which creators should be compensated for specific uses of their work.

Another innovative approach involves creating global databases that consolidate song rights information from various sources into one accessible platform. Such databases would allow PROs around the world to reference a single source of truth when distributing royalties—greatly simplifying international collections.

Furthermore, smart contracts enabled by blockchain technology could automate payments based on predefined criteria set within the contract code itself. When certain conditions are met—such as a song reaching a certain number of streams—a payment would automatically be triggered without manual intervention.

Lastly, user-centric payment models represent an innovative shift away from traditional pro-rata systems where all revenue goes into one pot before being divided among artists based on market share metrics. Instead, user-centric models allocate payments based on individual listener behavior— ensuring that subscription fees directly support the artists whom users actually listen to.

59

Greater Transparency for Creators

Transparency remains one of the most pressing demands from creators regarding royalty collections—and rightfully so; understanding where one's income comes from is fundamental to making informed career decisions as an artist.

One way transparency has been increased is through more detailed reporting from digital service providers (DSPs) and PROs alike. Many organizations now offer online portals where artists can track their streams and downloads in real-time along with corresponding revenue estimates.

Open-access policies have also emerged whereby some PROs publicly disclose payout rates per stream or download across different platforms— providing creators with clearer expectations about potential earnings from their work.

Creators are also pushing for "black box" income—the unattributed royalties collected but not yet paid out—to be dealt with more transparently by ensuring these funds are eventually paid out equitably rather than absorbed into general distributions favoring top-tier artists disproportionately.

In addition to technological solutions like blockchain providing immutable records accessible by all stakeholders involved in a piece's creation; legislative efforts such as The Music Modernization Act (MMA) passed in 2018 aim at improving transparency through reforms like establishing a mechanical licensing collective responsible for managing digital mechanical licenses more openly than ever before.

60

These advancements collectively signal progress towards empowering creators with knowledge about their creative output's financial performance while fostering trust between them and those tasked with managing their intellectual property rights effectively.

61

Chapter 13: Music Rights Management

Understanding Music Rights Management

The music industry is a labyrinth of creativity intertwined with legal complexities, and at the heart of this maze lies music rights management. This critical aspect of the industry ensures that those who create music—be it songwriters, composers, performers, or producers—are fairly compensated for their work when it is used or consumed by others.

Music rights management revolves around intellectual property (IP) laws that protect the interests of creators. These laws grant them exclusive rights to use and distribute their work and to authorize others to do the same in exchange for royalties. The types of royalties include mechanical royalties from physical sales and digital downloads; performance royalties from radio, TV broadcasts, and live performances; synchronization royalties from using music in film, TV shows, commercials, and video games; and print music royalties from sheet music sales.

In today's digital age, where streaming services dominate the market, tracking these various revenue streams has become more complex. Digital platforms have made it easier for music to reach global audiences but have also complicated royalty collection due to different countries having their own rules and rates for royalty payments.

62

To navigate this complexity, artists must register their works with multiple entities such as Performing Rights Organizations (PROs), mechanical rights agencies, and digital service providers. Each entity plays a role in collecting specific types of royalties. For instance, PROs like ASCAP or BMI collect performance royalties while mechanical rights agencies handle mechanical royalties.

Moreover, understanding how to correctly register works is paramount. Incorrect registration can lead to missed royalty payments or disputes over ownership. It requires meticulous attention to detail regarding metadata—the information that accompanies a musical composition or recording that includes titles, writer names, publisher details, ISRC codes for recordings, and other crucial data points.

Beyond registration lies the challenge of maximizing earnings. This involves not only understanding where your music is being played but also negotiating favorable deals with publishers or labels who can help manage your catalog effectively.

The future holds promise for simplifying these processes through emerging technologies like blockchain which offers potential solutions for transparently tracking usage across platforms globally. Artificial intelligence could further revolutionize royalty collection by automating identification and payment processes.

63

In essence, understanding music rights management is about recognizing the value of one's creative output and taking proactive steps to safeguard it within an ever-shifting digital landscape—a task requiring continuous learning and adaptation.

Role of Industry Experts

Industry experts play an indispensable role in shaping the careers of musicians by guiding them through the intricate web of music rights management. These professionals come from various backgrounds including law, business administration, publishing, A&R (Artists & Repertoire), and technology sectors—all converging on a common goal: ensuring creators receive fair compensation for their work.

Lawyers specializing in entertainment law are often at the forefront when dealing with contracts between artists and other parties such as record labels or publishers. They ensure that agreements are equitable and protect artists' interests over both short-term gains and long-term career sustainability.

Music publishers bring another layer of expertise by managing songwriters' catalogs—promoting songs to recording artists; securing synchronization licenses; collecting mechanical royalties; administering copyrights; negotiating deals; handling foreign sub-publishing arrangements —and thus playing a vital role in generating income for songwriters.

64

A&R professionals bridge creative talent with commercial opportunity by scouting new talent; nurturing artist development; overseeing production processes—and ultimately influencing what gets released into the market.

On the technological front are experts who develop systems for tracking usage across various media platforms worldwide—ensuring accurate royalty distribution through sophisticated software solutions that deal with metadata analysis among other things.

These industry veterans also serve as educators—sharing knowledge through seminars; workshops; writing books like "Music Royalty Collection Guide"; contributing articles—or even mentoring up-and-coming artists directly about best practices within the industry.

Furthermore they advocate on behalf of creators at policy-making levels— fighting for better copyright protection laws or fairer streaming payout models—which has significant implications on how revenues are generated within the industry as a whole.

Their collective experience provides invaluable insights into not just surviving but thriving within an industry characterized by rapid change due to technological advancements—a testament to their pivotal role in sustaining its economic vitality while championing artistic integrity.

65

Chapter 14: Empowering Independent Artists

Understanding the Intricacies of Music Royalty Collection

In the digital era, where music consumption has shifted from physical sales to streams and downloads, understanding how music royalties are collected is paramount for artists to ensure they receive their fair share of earnings. The collection of music royalties is a multifaceted process that involves various stakeholders and requires meticulous attention to detail.

Royalties are generated through different means: mechanical royalties from the reproduction of songs, performance royalties from public broadcasts, synchronization royalties from pairing music with visual media, and print music royalties from the sale of sheet music. Each type has its own method of collection and distribution, which can be complex due to the global nature of the music industry.

Mechanical royalties, for instance, are collected by mechanical rights organizations in each territory that license reproduction rights. These organizations then pay out to publishers and songwriters. Performance royalties are collected by Performing Rights Organizations (PROs) like ASCAP, BMI, or SESAC in the United States. They monitor radio plays, live performances, streaming services, and other public broadcasts to allocate payments accordingly.

66

Synchronization royalties occur when a song is used in conjunction with visual media such as movies, TV shows, commercials or video games. These are typically negotiated directly with the copyright holder or their representative and can vary greatly depending on factors like the prominence of the song's use and the size of the audience.

Print music royalties are less common in today's digital age but still relevant for composers who create works intended for live performance or educational purposes. These royalties come from sales of sheet music and scores.

The digital age has introduced new platforms like Spotify, Apple Music, YouTube, and others that require artists to understand how these services track usage and report it back for royalty distribution. Digital Service Providers (DSPs) have agreements with record labels and publishers to stream their content; however, independent artists must often navigate this landscape themselves or partner with aggregators who can place their music on these platforms.

To maximize earnings from these various sources—both domestic and international—artists need to register their works correctly with all relevant organizations. This includes not only PROs but also mechanical rights agencies and any other entities involved in collecting specific types of royalties.

67

Negotiating publishing deals is another critical aspect where knowledge is power. Understanding contract terms can prevent artists from signing away more rights than necessary or getting locked into unfavorable conditions. It's important for creators to recognize common pitfalls such as unclear royalty splits or clauses that limit future income potential.

Real-world examples abound where artists have either missed out on significant earnings due to a lack of understanding about royalty collection or have successfully navigated these waters to maximize their revenue. For instance, independent musicians who meticulously register their works across all platforms often see greater returns than those who overlook this crucial step.

Emerging Technologies Shaping Future Royalties

The future landscape of music royalty collection looks promising thanks to emerging technologies like blockchain and artificial intelligence (AI). These innovations hold potential for revolutionizing how creators track usage rights and collect earnings by offering enhanced transparency and efficiency.

Blockchain technology could transform royalty collection by creating a decentralized ledger that tracks ownership rights transparently across every transaction involving a piece of work. This would allow real-time tracking of how content is being used worldwide while ensuring accurate payment distribution among all parties involved.

68

Artificial intelligence also offers exciting possibilities in identifying uses of copyrighted material across various media outlets more efficiently than ever before. AI algorithms can scour vast amounts of data on streaming platforms or social media channels to detect unlicensed uses quickly so that appropriate action can be taken.

These technologies could streamline processes that currently involve multiple intermediaries—such as PROs—and reduce administrative overhead costs associated with royalty collection. By doing so, they promise faster payouts directly into creators' pockets while minimizing errors in reporting usage statistics.

However, implementing these technologies comes with challenges such as ensuring widespread adoption within an industry known for its complexity regarding rights management systems already in place. Moreover, there will be legal hurdles related to copyright law adjustments needed to accommodate new ways of managing intellectual property rights digitally.

Despite these challenges though some startups have begun experimenting with blockchain-based solutions aimed at simplifying royalty collections—for example Audius—a decentralized platform designed specifically for musicians looking for more control over their content distribution without intermediaries taking cuts along the way.

69

As we move forward into an increasingly digitized world where traditional models continue evolving rapidly under technological advancements pressure—it becomes clear why staying informed about developments affecting future revenue streams remains essential anyone serious about making living off artistry today's economy. In conclusion understanding intricacies behind current practices coupled anticipation changes horizon empowers independent artists take charge financial destiny armed knowledge tools necessary succeed amidst shifting sands modern-day musical commerce landscape

70

Chapter 15: Making a Living from Art in the Digital Economy

Understanding Music Royalty Collection in the Digital Age

The digital age has revolutionized the way music is consumed, leading to a seismic shift in how royalties are collected and distributed. In this era of streaming services and downloads, it's imperative for artists to understand the nuances of music royalty collection to ensure they receive fair compensation for their work. The landscape is complex, with various types of royalties such as mechanical, performance, synchronization, and print music royalties.

Mechanical royalties are generated when a song is reproduced and distributed physically or digitally. With the decline of physical sales and the rise of streaming platforms like Spotify and Apple Music, these royalties have become predominantly stream-centric. Performance royalties occur when a song is played publicly, whether on radio stations, in venues, or through online broadcasts. Synchronization royalties come into play when music is used in conjunction with visual media – think movies, TV shows, commercials, or video games.

In today's digital economy, artists must register their works with Performing Rights Organizations (PROs) like ASCAP or BMI to track performances and collect due royalties. These organizations monitor usage across various platforms and ensure that artists are compensated for their creative output.

71

Moreover, understanding contracts and publishing deals is crucial. Many artists lose out on potential earnings by not negotiating terms that favor their long-term financial interests. It's essential to recognize common pitfalls in contracts that can hinder royalty collection.

The future also holds promise with emerging technologies such as blockchain offering potential solutions for more transparent and efficient royalty distribution systems. Blockchain could enable real-time tracking of music consumption and direct payment to rights holders, minimizing discrepancies in royalty collection.

Artists need to stay informed about these developments while also leveraging traditional knowledge about rights management to maximize their earnings from both domestic and international sources. By doing so, they can transform what might seem like an overwhelming challenge into a manageable aspect of their careers.

Maximizing Earnings from Domestic and International Royalties

To fully capitalize on one's creative work requires a strategic approach to collecting both domestic and international royalties. Artists often focus on local markets but overlook the potential revenue from global streams and performances. To tap into this income stream effectively requires registering with multiple PROs around the world or working with sub-publishers who can manage international collections.

72

One key strategy involves understanding reciprocal agreements between different countries' PROs which ensure that artists receive royalties from abroad just as they would at home. This global network functions as a web connecting various territories so that an artist's public performance in one country results in them being paid by their home PRO.

Additionally, there are mechanical rights organizations such as Harry Fox Agency in the U.S., which handle mechanical licensing for physical copies and digital downloads internationally. For synchronization rights involving film or advertising abroad, it may be beneficial to work directly with specialized agents who understand regional market specifics.

It's also important for artists to be aware of differing copyright laws across countries which can affect how long they earn royalties after initial publication; some regions offer protection for 50 years post-publication while others extend up to 70 years or more.

Real-world examples abound where artists have either succeeded spectacularly or failed miserably at securing international royalties due simply to awareness (or lack thereof) regarding these mechanisms. Success stories often involve proactive engagement with foreign markets through touring or targeted marketing campaigns alongside robust registration practices ensuring all possible revenue streams are tapped into efficiently.

73

Negotiating Publishing Deals & Understanding Contracts

When entering publishing deals or signing contracts related to music rights management, clarity is paramount—both parties must fully understand terms concerning advances, recoupment policies, ownership splits between songwriter(s) and publisher(s), duration of agreements among other critical factors before finalizing any agreement.

A well-negotiated contract should balance immediate financial needs against long-term career goals; it should provide fair advance payments without imposing restrictive recoupment conditions which could stifle future earnings potential if not carefully considered beforehand.

Artists should seek legal advice when necessary especially if unfamiliar terminology arises during negotiations; having an experienced lawyer review contract details can prevent misunderstandings later down the line potentially saving thousands if not millions.

78

Chapter 16: Essential Knowledge for Musicians

Music Royalty Collection in the Digital Age

The digital age has revolutionized the way music is consumed, distributed, and monetized. With the advent of streaming services like Spotify, Apple Music, and YouTube, the traditional revenue streams for musicians have shifted dramatically. In this context, understanding how music royalties are collected in the digital realm is paramount for artists to ensure they receive fair compensation for their work.

Royalties in the digital age are primarily generated through streams and downloads. Each time a song is played on a streaming service or purchased online, it generates income for the rights holders. However, unlike physical sales where royalties are relatively straightforward, digital platforms involve complex algorithms and agreements that determine how much money an artist makes per play.

To navigate this complexity, musicians must familiarize themselves with digital service providers (DSPs) and how they operate. DSPs have licensing agreements with record labels and music publishers to use their catalogs. These agreements define royalty rates which can vary widely depending on factors such as user subscription fees, advertising revenue, and country-specific streaming rates.

79

Moreover, artists need to understand the role of aggregators—companies that act as intermediaries between independent artists and DSPs. Aggregators help distribute music to various platforms and collect royalties on behalf of artists for a fee or percentage of earnings.

One significant challenge in the digital age is data management. With millions of streams happening worldwide every day, accurately tracking plays and ensuring correct royalty payments can be daunting. This has led to innovations such as blockchain technology being explored as a means to create more transparent and efficient royalty distribution systems.

In addition to technological solutions, artists should also consider joining Performing Rights Organizations (PROs). PROs collect performance royalties whenever music is played publicly—whether live at a venue or broadcasted over radio or TV—and distribute them to songwriters and publishers.

Understanding these mechanisms is crucial for musicians who wish to thrive financially in today's music industry landscape. By staying informed about changes in digital distribution models and leveraging available technologies and organizations designed to protect their interests, artists can better manage their creative income streams.

80

Negotiating Publishing Deals

Securing a favorable publishing deal can significantly impact an artist's career trajectory. A good deal not only provides upfront financial benefits but also ensures long-term earnings through effective management of an artist's catalog.

When negotiating publishing deals, it's essential for musicians to grasp what rights they are signing away and what they retain. Typically, a publisher will want ownership or administration rights over an artist's compositions which allows them to license the music for use in various media such as films or commercials (sync licenses), generating additional income through synchronization royalties.

Artists should approach negotiations with clear goals regarding advance payments (if any), royalty splits between songwriter(s) and publisher(s), duration of the agreement, territory coverage (domestic vs international), reversion clauses that allow rights to revert back after certain conditions are met, creative control over how songs are used commercially among other terms.

It's advisable for musicians to seek legal counsel before entering into any contracts; experienced entertainment lawyers can provide valuable insights into industry standards and help negotiate better terms. Additionally, understanding common contract pitfalls—such as unclear definitions of net receipts or ambiguous language around deductions—can prevent future disputes over royalty calculations.

81

Real-world examples abound where artists have either benefited from well-negotiated deals or suffered due to unfavorable terms. For instance, some legacy acts have successfully renegotiated their contracts thanks to increased leverage from sustained popularity over time while others have had their works tied up due to restrictive long-term contracts signed early in their careers without proper guidance.

By being well-informed about publishing deal structures and maintaining realistic expectations while negotiating assertively yet fairly with potential partners will position artists favorably within these critical business arrangements.

Emerging Technologies: Blockchain & Artificial Intelligence

The future of music royalties looks promising with emerging technologies like blockchain and artificial intelligence poised to revolutionize collection processes by enhancing transparency and efficiency across the board.

Blockchain technology offers a decentralized ledger system where transactions (in this case musical plays/downloads) can be recorded securely without central authority intervention thus reducing opportunities for errors or fraud during royalty distributions; smart contracts programmed into blockchains could automatically execute payments when certain conditions are met streamlining administrative tasks considerably reducing overhead costs associated with traditional collection methods allowing creators to receive dues faster than ever before.

84

Chapter 17: Staying Current with Industry Standards

Understanding the Intricacies of Music Royalty Collection

In the realm of music, royalties are the lifeblood that sustains creators, allowing them to reap financial benefits from their art. The collection of music royalties has become a complex affair in the digital era, where traditional revenue streams have been supplanted by downloads and streaming services. To fully grasp this intricate system, one must understand the various types of royalties and how they are generated.

Mechanical royalties originate from the reproduction of songs, such as when a track is downloaded or physically produced on CDs and vinyl. Performance royalties are accrued when a song is played publicly, whether it's through radio broadcasts, live performances, or streamed over internet platforms. Synchronization royalties come into play when music is used in conjunction with visual media like films, TV shows, or advertisements. Lastly, print music royalties are earned through the sale of sheet music and songbooks.

The digital age has revolutionized how these royalties are collected and distributed. With streaming services becoming ubiquitous, mechanical and performance royalties have seen significant changes in their collection processes. Digital Service Providers (DSPs) like Spotify and Apple Music negotiate with record labels and publishers to determine royalty rates for streams—a process often criticized for its lack of transparency.

85

To navigate this landscape effectively, artists must register their works with PROs—organizations responsible for tracking performances and collecting royalties on behalf of songwriters and composers. These entities play a crucial role in ensuring that artists receive payment whenever their music is played across various platforms.

However, registration alone isn't enough; musicians must also understand how to maximize their earnings through both domestic and international channels. This involves leveraging reciprocal agreements between different countries' PROs to collect worldwide performance royalties—an essential step for artists looking to expand their global reach.

Negotiating publishing deals can be another avenue for maximizing royalty income. A well-negotiated contract can secure favorable terms for an artist regarding advances, royalty rates, and ownership rights over their work. Understanding contractual language is vital to avoid common pitfalls that may lead to lost revenue or legal disputes.

Real-world examples abound where artists have either succeeded in optimizing their royalty collections or fallen victim to oversight. Take the case of an independent musician who diligently registered her songs with a PRO but neglected to affiliate herself as a publisher as well—resulting in only half the potential performance royalties being collected until she rectified this oversight.

86

As we look toward future technologies like blockchain and artificial intelligence (AI), there's potential for even greater efficiency in royalty collection processes. Blockchain technology promises enhanced transparency by creating immutable records of ownership and transactions—potentially simplifying licensing agreements and reducing disputes over payments. AI could automate many aspects of royalty collection, identifying usage patterns more quickly than humanly possible.

In conclusion, understanding music royalty collection requires not only knowledge of current practices but also foresight into technological advancements that may reshape industry standards.

Maximizing Earnings from Domestic and International Sources

For musicians seeking financial sustainability through their craft, maximizing earnings from both domestic and international sources is paramount. In today's interconnected world where music transcends borders at the click of a button, tapping into international markets can significantly boost an artist's income stream.

Domestically speaking, artists should ensure they're registered with all relevant PROs within their home country to capture all potential performance revenues—from radio airplay to live venue performances. Additionally, securing distribution deals that cover multiple platforms can increase mechanical royalty earnings from downloads and physical sales alike.

87

Internationally however things get more complex due to varying copyright laws across different jurisdictions which affect how much money makes its way back to creators' pockets after foreign plays or sales occur abroad; hence why having knowledge about reciprocal agreements between PROs worldwide becomes critical here since these partnerships facilitate cross-border payments among member organizations thus allowing artists access broader audiences without sacrificing rightful compensation due them under law wherever they may reside globally speaking .

Moreover negotiating direct licensing deals outside one's own country might prove beneficial especially if dealing directly with foreign entities such as labels or distributors who have better insights into local markets thereby potentially offering more lucrative terms than what might be available domestically speaking . Case studies show numerous instances where bands have successfully leveraged fan bases overseas leading not only increased revenue streams but also opportunities tour internationally further expanding brand recognition while simultaneously generating additional income via merchandise sales concert tickets etcetera .

Furthermore understanding cultural nuances market trends specific regions plays key role determining best strategies employ when attempting penetrate new territories musically . For instance genres popular certain areas may differ greatly compared others meaning adaptation approach necessary order resonate local listenership effectively .

88

Lastly staying abreast changes within international copyright legislation remains essential part equation given ongoing debates surrounding fair remuneration digital age particularly concerning streaming payouts which continue evolve rapidly pace making it imperative keep informed latest developments ensure one's interests adequately protected times .

In essence maximizing earnings from domestic international sources entails strategic planning thorough research proactive engagement diverse markets—all aimed at establishing sustainable profitable career within ever-changing landscape global music industry.

Negotiating Publishing Deals

When it comes down negotiating publishing deals knowledge power . A good deal can provide financial security creative freedom whereas bad one lead years frustration missed opportunities . It starts understanding basic elements involved including advances recoupment clauses royalty percentages term lengths rights reversion policies among other factors .

Advances upfront payments made publisher songwriter exchange future earnings typically recouped before any additional paid out meaning higher advance isn't always better especially if unlikely earn back amount given time frame stipulated agreement . Recoupment clauses detail exactly what expenses will deducted overall gross income prior calculating net payable artist so clarity here crucial avoiding surprises down line .

89

Royalty percentages vary depending type right being licensed example mechanical versus synchronization rights each carrying its own standard rate industry however room negotiation exists based perceived value work question bargaining position parties involved . Term length refers duration contract itself longer terms usually favor publishers since allows them exploit works extended period time shorter ones benefit songwriters composers giving them opportunity renegotiate sooner should circumstances change favorably towards them .

Rights reversion policy outlines conditions under which control over copyrighted material returns original owner after certain milestones met such expiration initial term fulfillment contractual obligations etcetera making sure clear path laid out regaining full ownership important aspect consider during negotiations prevent getting locked perpetually unfavorable arrangements .

Case study illustrating importance savvy deal-making would involve independent singer-songwriter managed secure 100% retention his publishing despite receiving smaller advance return demonstrating willingness take risk betting himself long run rather than opting immediate payout expense losing control artistic output perpetuity .

90

Ultimately successful negotiation hinges upon thorough preparation willingness walk away table if necessary confidence advocate oneself interests above all else ensuring fair equitable outcome achieved end day benefiting all stakeholders involved process equally.

Emerging Technologies: Blockchain & Artificial Intelligence

The advent emerging technologies blockchain artificial intelligence poised revolutionize way we think about manage distribute collect music royalties offering unprecedented levels transparency efficiency previously unattainable traditional systems currently place .

Blockchain essentially decentralized ledger technology capable recording transactions securely immutably meaning once data entered cannot altered tampered with any way providing perfect solution longstanding issues related tracking usage licensing agreements payment distributions within context copyright management because every transaction recorded chain visible verifiable anyone network eliminating need trust third-party intermediaries handle these matters behalf creators users alike thereby cutting costs speeding up entire process significantly .

Artificial intelligence on other hand brings automation scale analyzing vast amounts data identify patterns behaviors useful predicting trends optimizing decision-making processes example AI-powered algorithms could deployed monitor radio stations streaming services social media platforms detect instances copyrighted content being used without proper authorization then automatically initiate claims recovery procedures behalf owners saving time effort manual monitoring enforcement activities traditionally required carry out same tasks effectively freeing up resources focus creative endeavors instead administrative ones ultimately leading higher productivity profitability long-term perspective .

91

Real-world applications already underway companies developing solutions harness power these cutting-edge tools streamline operations across board case point startup utilizing blockchain create smart contracts automatically execute terms agreed upon parties involved transaction e.g., releasing funds once certain conditions fulfilled verifying authenticity ownership works question before granting licenses use commercially another using machine learning techniques analyze listener preferences tailor recommendations accordingly increasing chances discovery consumption thereby driving up associated revenues process overall trend clear direction moving forward integration innovation key staying ahead curve competitive fast-paced environment characterizes modern-day music business landscape today tomorrow beyond .

92

Chapter 18: Conclusion - Unlocking the Secrets Behind Creative Income

Understanding the Intricacies of Music Royalty Collection

In the realm of music, royalties are the lifeblood that sustains creators, allowing them to reap financial benefits from their art. The collection of music royalties is a nuanced process that requires both knowledge and vigilance. At its core, understanding music royalty collection involves grasping the different types of royalties available to artists, including mechanical, performance, synchronization, and print music royalties.

Mechanical royalties are generated when a musical composition is reproduced in physical or digital form. With the advent of streaming services like Spotify and Apple Music, these royalties have become more complex to track due to the sheer volume of data involved in digital reproductions. Performance royalties arise when a song is played publicly—whether on radio stations, in concert venues, or through online platforms. Synchronization royalties occur when music is used in conjunction with visual media such as films, television shows, or advertisements. Lastly, print music royalties are earned through the sale of sheet music and other printed musical scores.

93

The key to unlocking these revenue streams lies in proper registration with relevant organizations such as Performing Rights Organizations (PROs), which collect performance royalties on behalf of songwriters and publishers. Similarly, mechanical licenses and synchronization deals require meticulous attention to detail to ensure fair compensation.

In today's digital age where metadata plays a crucial role in tracking usage across various platforms, it's imperative for artists to understand how their information is managed and shared among industry players. This includes ensuring that ISRC (International Standard Recording Code) and other identifiers are correctly attached to their work so that every stream or download can be accurately monetized.

Moreover, musicians must stay informed about international royalty collection practices since digital distribution often leads to global exposure. Different countries may have unique systems for collecting and distributing music royalties; therefore, having an international strategy can significantly enhance an artist's earning potential.

Negotiating publishing deals also forms a critical part of maximizing income from music rights. Artists need to be aware of common contractual pitfalls that could limit their earnings or tie up their rights unnecessarily. By understanding contract terms and seeking legal advice when necessary, creators can better protect their interests and ensure they receive fair compensation for their work.

94

Real-world examples abound where artists have either succeeded in optimizing their royalty collections or failed due to lack of knowledge or oversight. For instance, independent musicians who meticulously register their works with all relevant bodies often see greater returns than those who overlook this crucial step.

As we look toward the future with emerging technologies like blockchain promising more transparency and efficiency in royalty collection processes, it's essential for artists to stay abreast of these developments. Blockchain technology has the potential to revolutionize how rights are managed by creating immutable records for each transaction related to a piece of music —potentially simplifying licensing agreements and reducing disputes over ownership.

In conclusion, understanding the intricacies behind music royalty collection is not just about knowing what types of revenues exist but also mastering how they are tracked, collected, and maximized across different mediums and borders. It requires continuous education on industry standards as well as staying informed about technological advancements that could impact future earnings.

Maximizing Earnings from Domestic and International Sources 95

For musicians looking to maximize their creative income from both domestic and international sources effectively navigating through complex networks is essential. Domestically within countries like the United States PROs such as ASCAP BMI SESAC play pivotal roles collecting performance-related revenues on behalf artists composers publishers alike However beyond borders complexities multiply Understanding differing copyright laws varying operational structures foreign PROs becomes paramount success global market

One strategy enhancing international earnings involves directly registering works multiple territories rather than relying solely upon one's home country PRO facilitate collections This proactive approach ensures broader coverage potentially increases overall revenue especially important given disparities rates between countries Additionally establishing relationships sub-publishers local representatives can aid navigating foreign markets securing better deals

Furthermore leveraging digital platforms' global reach presents another avenue increasing visibility hence potential earnings Digital Service Providers DSPs offer unprecedented access audiences worldwide but also require understanding nuances algorithm-driven promotion distribution Ensuring one's content optimized platform-specific requirements engaging actively social media help boost streams downloads thereby increasing associated revenues

96

Case studies illustrate importance being proactive internationally For example independent artist who took time build fanbase Japan saw significant spike sales streams after touring region collaborating local acts Conversely band neglected register songs properly missed out thousands dollars due uncollected performance royalties overseas

Ultimately maximizing earnings domestic international sources demands strategic approach informed decisions based thorough research networking While daunting task outset resources guides available assist navigating this terrain With right tools support even indie artists carve out lucrative careers global stage

Negotiating Publishing Deals Understanding Contracts

When entering into publishing deals comprehending contract terms cannot overstated A well-negotiated deal can provide substantial income security while poor agreement might restrict artist's career growth limit financial opportunities Key aspects consider include advances royalty rates recoupment policies term length ownership rights

Advances upfront payments made publisher songwriter exchange future earnings These funds allow artists focus creating without immediate financial pressure however they typically recouped against future royalties meaning no additional payouts occur until advance paid back fully Understanding implications recoupment vital avoid unpleasant surprises down line

97

Royalty rates determine percentage sales revenue allocated creator They vary widely depending type deal individual bargaining power It's crucial negotiate highest possible rate consistent market standards Additionally clauses addressing rate adjustments based sales milestones beneficial ensuring fair compensation long-term

Term length refers duration agreement Shorter terms offer flexibility renegotiate sooner potentially advantageous changing market conditions Longer contracts however might come higher advances stability but risk locking unfavorable terms longer period Weighing pros cons based personal career goals essential making informed decision

Ownership rights pertain control over works post-contractual period Retaining certain degree ownership allows continued earning potential even after initial deal expires Conversely transferring full ownership means relinquishing all future claims work Negotiating favorable balance between immediate gains long-term benefits key successful contract

Real-world anecdotes abound illustrating consequences good bad negotiation tactics Anecdotal evidence suggests many young inexperienced musicians sign away significant portions rights little return due lack understanding pressure succeed quickly On flip side savvy negotiators leverage experience reputation secure advantageous deals set precedent others industry follow

98

In essence negotiating publishing deals understanding contracts involves careful consideration numerous factors Armed knowledge legal counsel if necessary creators position themselves advantageously within competitive landscape Ultimately goal should always strike balance between short-term gains sustainable long-term success

Emerging Technologies Streamlining Royalty Collection Processes

The intersection emerging technologies traditional royalty collection processes holds promise revolutionizing way creators compensated

Innovations blockchain artificial intelligence AI poised streamline operations increase transparency entire ecosystem Blockchain particular offers decentralized ledger system where transactions recorded chronologically publicly This feature could simplify licensing agreements reduce disputes over ownership by providing clear traceable record every use piece music Moreover smart contracts self-executing contracts predefined rules coded into them automate payments once conditions met eliminating need manual processing thus speeding up distribution funds

AI also plays growing role analyzing vast amounts data predict trends optimize pricing strategies For instance machine learning algorithms analyze streaming patterns suggest optimal release times promotional efforts tailored specific audiences Furthermore AI-driven tools assist identifying instances copyright infringement online enabling swifter action against unauthorized uses works

99

These technologies not only promise improve accuracy efficiency but also empower artists greater control over intellectual property By reducing reliance intermediaries direct-to-fan models become viable allowing fans support favorite musicians directly cutting out middlemen costs associated traditional distribution channels

However adoption new technologies comes challenges skepticism resistance change among established players concerns regarding privacy security Nonetheless forward-thinking individuals organizations embracing potential reshape industry benefit all stakeholders involved As technology continues evolve keeping pace innovations will increasingly important part maintaining thriving career arts sector

To sum up emerging technologies hold key unlocking next level efficiency transparency within world music royalty collection While still early days adoption widespread implementation these tools could herald new era empowerment fairness creative industries Embracing change adapting swiftly will enable current future generations artists thrive ever-changing landscape

"Music Royalty Collection Guide" is an essential resource for individuals in the music industry seeking to understand the complexities of music royalty collection in the digital era. The book offers a comprehensive look at the various types of royalties, including mechanical, performance, synchronization, and print music royalties, and how they are generated through streams and downloads.

The guide begins with a historical perspective on music publishing and its evolution due to technological advancements. It then navigates readers through the current music rights landscape, introducing key stakeholders such as Performing Rights Organizations (PROs), record labels, music publishers, and digital service providers.

Key points include detailed instructions on registering works to ensure accurate royalty collection and distribution, strategies for maximizing earnings from both domestic and international sources, and advice on negotiating publishing deals and understanding contracts. The book also warns of common pitfalls that can hinder artists from receiving their rightful earnings.

Notable insights are provided through real-world examples and case studies that illustrate how theoretical concepts apply in practice. Additionally, "Music Royalty Collection Guide" looks ahead to the future impact of emerging technologies like blockchain and artificial intelligence on royalty collection processes.

Written by industry experts with extensive experience in music rights management, this guide serves as both an educational tool for newcomers and a reference manual for seasoned professionals aiming to keep up with industry standards and best practices.

In summary, this book empowers readers with knowledge to transform what may seem like an overwhelming task into a manageable one. It is designed to be an indispensable asset for anyone serious about earning a living from their art in today's digital economy.